W9-CGL-446

Ireland

Written by

Neil Grant

Consultant J. Lynch

Illustrated by

Borin van Loon and Ann Savage

SILVER BURDETT PRESS

ENGLEWOOD CLIFFS, NEW JERSEY

U.S. Project Editor Nancy Furstinger
U.S. Editor Ruth Marsh
Editor Caroline White
Designer Robert Mathias, Publishing Workshop
Photo-researcher Hugh Olliff

A TEMPLAR BOOK

Devised and produced by Templar Publishing Ltd
Pippbrook Mill, London Road, Dorking, Surrey RH4 1JE

Adapted and first published in the United States in 1989
by Silver Burdett Press, Englewood Cliffs, N.J.

Color separations by Positive Colour Ltd, Maldon, Essex
Printed by L.E.G.O., Vicenza, Italy

Library of Congress Cataloging-in-Publication Data

Grant, Neil.
    Ireland / written by Neil Grant; consultant, J. Lynch.—U.S. ed.
        p. cm. — (People & places)
    "A Templar book."
    Includes index.
    Summary: Introduces the geography, history, people, and
culture of the Emerald Isle.
    1. Ireland—Juvenile literature.   2. Northern Ireland—Juvenile
    literature. [1. Ireland.   2. Northern Ireland.]   I. Title.
    II. Series: People & places (Englewood Cliffs, N.J.)
    DA906.G7   1989
    941.6—dc 19   89-4307
    ISBN 0-382-09819-6   CIP
                                                  AC

Contents

ON THE EDGE OF EUROPE

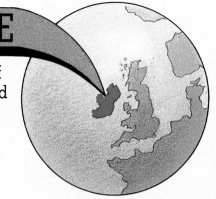

Ireland is a large island on the western edge of Europe. It is separated from the even larger island of Great Britain by the Irish Sea, which is only 14 miles wide at the narrowest point. To the north, west, and south of Ireland is the Atlantic Ocean.

For hundreds of years Ireland was ruled by the British. Since 1921 it has been divided into the independent Republic of Ireland, and Northern Ireland, which is still part of the United Kingdom. Today Britain and the Republic of Ireland are allies, and there are close links between British and Irish people. Irish citizens are allowed to live and work in Britain if they choose. There they have the same rights as British subjects, including the right to vote. Yet relations between the two governments are not always as warm as they might be. The memory of British rule, and the fact that part of Ireland is still British, cause problems between the two countries.

In the past, many Irish people left the country, looking for a better life. A large number came to the United States, where their Irish-American descendants live today. This gives Ireland a special link with the United States.

National emblem
The shamrock is a national emblem of Ireland. According to legend, St. Patrick (the patron saint of Ireland who converted the Irish to Christianity) used the shamrock in a sermon to help explain the idea of the Holy Trinity.

Flags of Ireland

Flag of the Republic of Ireland

The national flag of Ireland is of three colors; green, the color of the old Irish clans; white, the color of peace; and orange, the color of the province of Ulster. Most of Ulster is in Northern Ireland, and the white stripe is a sign of hope for peace between the "Orange" and the "Green." The flag of Ulster bears a red hand, which is the ancient symbol of Ulster.

Flag of Ulster

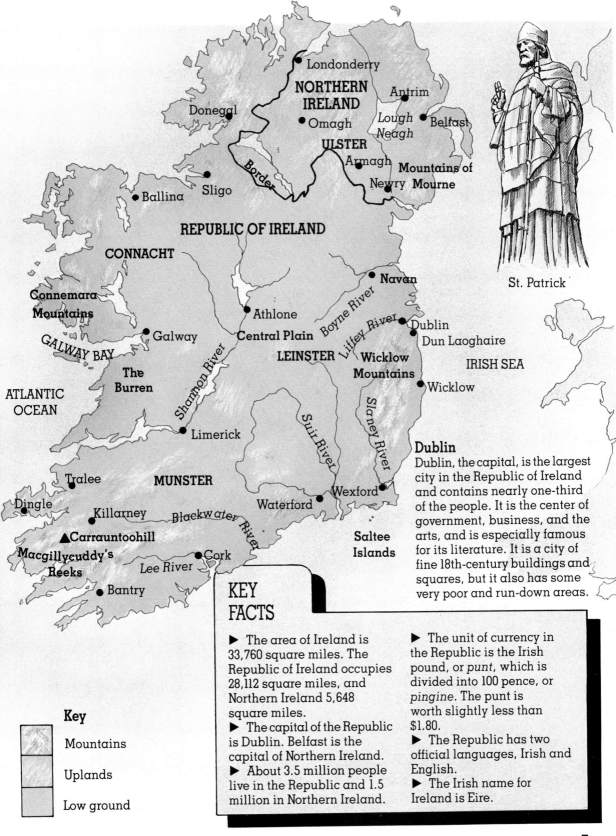

Londonderry

**NORTHERN
IRELAND**

Antrim

Donegal

*Lough
Neagh*

Belfast

Omagh

ULSTER

Armagh

Border

Newry

**Mountains of
Mourne**

Ballina

Sligo

REPUBLIC OF IRELAND

CONNACHT

Navan

**Connemara
Mountains**

Athlone

Boyne River

Liffey River

Dublin

GALWAY BAY

Galway

Central Plain

Dun Laoghaire

LEINSTER

IRISH SEA

**ATLANTIC
OCEAN**

**The
Burren**

Shannon River

**Wicklow
Mountains**

Suir River

Slaney River

Wicklow

Limerick

MUNSTER

Tralee

Wexford

Dingle

Waterford

Killarney

Blackwater River

**Saltee
Islands**

▲Carrauntoohill

**Macgillycuddy's
Reeks**

Cork

Lee River

Bantry

St. Patrick

Dublin

Dublin, the capital, is the largest
city in the Republic of Ireland
and contains nearly one-third
of the people. It is the center of
government, business, and the
arts, and is especially famous
for its literature. It is a city of
fine 18th-century buildings and
squares, but it also has some
very poor and run-down areas.

KEY FACTS

▶ The area of Ireland is
33,760 square miles. The
Republic of Ireland occupies
28,112 square miles, and
Northern Ireland 5,648
square miles.
▶ The capital of the Republic
is Dublin. Belfast is the
capital of Northern Ireland.
▶ About 3.5 million people
live in the Republic and 1.5
million in Northern Ireland.

▶ The unit of currency in
the Republic is the Irish
pound, or *punt*, which is
divided into 100 pence, or
pingine. The punt is
worth slightly less than
$1.80.
▶ The Republic has two
official languages, Irish and
English.
▶ The Irish name for
Ireland is Eire.

Key

Mountains

Uplands

Low ground

7

EMERALD ISLE

Ireland is known as the Emerald Isle. Lush green grasslands cover much of the country, helped by the damp climate. On the western coast it is very wet, with up to 79 inches of rain a year. The famous bogs — wet, swampy areas of land — are the results of this heavy rainfall. The rest of the country, however, is not so rainy. A warm current from the Atlantic Ocean keeps Ireland mild in winter. Summers are cool, and fog is common.

The land of Ireland is shaped something like a saucer, with a flat plain in the middle, surrounded by mountains. Parts of the central plain are so waterlogged that farming is impossible, but many of the bogs have been drained in the past 50 years. Little remains of the forests that once covered much of the country.

The mountains are mostly low, but in the west there are steep, rugged ranges, and cliffs 660 feet high. Southwest of Dublin is a mountainous region, including the Wicklow Mountains, with deep valleys cut by glaciers long ago and peaks nearly 3,300 feet high.

Irish rivers usually run slowly and sometimes flow through lakes (*loughs*) and marshes. Rivers that flow down the mountains to the sea run more rapidly.

KEY FACTS

▶ In prehistoric times Ireland was probably joined to Britain at two places, Scotland in the north and Wales in the south.

▶ The Shannon River is 238 miles long, longer than any other river in Ireland.

▶ The highest point in Ireland is Carrauntoohill (3,412 feet), in Macgillycuddy's Reeks, in the southwest.

▶ In Ireland the wind usually blows from the southwest, bringing damp air from the Atlantic Ocean. In some parts summer is wetter than winter.

▶ Ireland has mild winters and cool summers. The average temperature in January is about 42°F. In July it is about 59°F.

▶ Rainfall is not heavy, but it is frequent. Wet days (with at least a shower) are more common than dry days.

The central plain
Here the land is fairly flat, with few hills over 650 feet above sea level. Most of the oak forests that once covered this land were cleared for pasture long ago.

Beautiful scenery

Ireland is famous for its beautiful scenery, especially in the west. In the southwestern corner, the mountains stretch out into the Atlantic, with long, deep inlets between them. The scenery is a mixture of rugged rocks, soft green valleys, and quiet bays. Many islands lie off the coast.

A fertile land

Much of Ireland is fertile, though much land consists of bog or mountain. Most of the fertile land is used for pasture and to produce hay (dried grass). Cows can graze outside for 10 months of the year because of the rich grass and mild climate.

FOUR PROVINCES

Ireland is divided into four provinces, which are named after ancient Irish kingdoms. They are Leinster in the east, Munster in the south, Connacht (or Connaught) in the west, and Ulster in the north. Each province is divided into counties, of which there are 32 altogether.

People often speak of Northern Ireland as "Ulster," although three of Ulster's nine counties, Donegal, Cavan, and Monaghan, are in the Republic.

About half the population of the Republic lives in Leinster, which contains the capital, Dublin. With more than 900,000 people, Dublin is the largest city; Belfast in Northern Ireland is the second largest.

Munster, though larger in area than Leinster, has only half as many people. It contains the Republic's second most important city, Cork.

Connacht is the smallest province, with the fewest people, but it is the most "Irish." Many people there still speak Irish as their first language, although they can speak English as well. The area where Irish is the chief spoken language is called the Gaeltacht.

For many years people from the country districts of Ireland have left the land to find work in cities, within Ireland, in Britain, and in other countries. People who worked the land often did not own their farms, and did not make enough money to support themselves. The movement of people to the cities is still going on. Villages and country towns are small, especially in the west, but the cities keep growing.

Lough Neagh

Lying in the center of Northern Ireland, Lough Neagh's shores touch five of the six Northern counties. It is the largest lake in Ireland, nearly 160 square miles in area and 98 feet deep in parts. According to legend, Lough Neagh arose suddenly from a fountain and covered many buildings, the remains of which are still there, far below the surface.

Cork

The center of Cork is on an island made by two branches of the Lee River. With its fine harbor, its 17th-century butter market, and its film festival (held in October every year) Cork attracts many visitors. It has been an industrial center since Henry Ford built the first tractor factory in Europe there 70 years ago, but it still has the look of a 19th-century city.

The four provinces

The four provinces of modern Ireland divide the country roughly into quarters: Ulster in the north, Leinster in the east, Munster in the south, and Connacht in the west. Although they are quarters, or "fourths," they are called by the Irish word meaning "fifths," because they are descended from the ancient Irish kingdoms known as "the five fifths." At that time, Leinster was divided into two kingdoms, North and South Leinster, which made five kingdoms altogether.

WILDLIFE AND LEPRECHAUNS

The wild animals and plants of Ireland are like those of neighboring Britain. Deer are the largest animals found there. They roam wild in the hills, protected from hunters by law.

Once there were giant Irish deer, as well as bears and wild boar. They all disappeared long ago, but wolves existed until the 1780s.

Ireland has some special varieties of wildlife, such as the Irish hare, Kerry slug, red grouse, and plenty of rabbits and foxes. In general, however, Ireland does not have very many wild animals. Many creatures common in other countries are not found in Ireland, such as the dormouse, certain kinds of bats, and most reptiles. There are no snakes in Ireland. No one knows why, although legends say that snakes were banished from the land by St. Patrick. Some very rare and beautiful wildflowers grow in Ireland, mainly in the west.

In folk stories Ireland is the land of pixies and leprechauns. These magical creatures add a touch of mystery to the countryside. A 19th-century Donegal poet, William Allingham, wrote in *The Fairies* (1850):

The Burren
South of Galway Bay lies the strange landscape of the Burren, nearly 400 square miles of bare, cracked limestone rock and windy hills. A 17th-century English general said of the region that there is "not enough earth to bury a man, nor wood to hang him, nor water to drown him." Yet many different wildflowers grow there because the rocks absorb heat and keep the scanty soil warm even in winter.

Up the airy mountain,
Down the rushy glen,
We daren't go a-hunting
For fear of little men.

William Allingham

12

Native animals and birds

Some kinds of animals are special to Ireland. The big lakes contain several fish of the char family not found anywhere else. Among birds, the coaltit and the jay are different from the U.S. varieties.

The Irish hare is like the mountain hare of Scotland, but has a redder coat in summer and, in winter, it sometimes becomes a piebald (covered with two-color patches) color.

Jay

Coaltit

Irish hare

Visiting seabirds

Many different seabirds visit the south and west coasts on their way to and from the European mainland. Ireland's largest bird sanctuary is on the Saltee Islands, off the Wexford coast in the southeast. There one can see the rare roseate tern, as well as puffins (right), gannets, petrels, Greenland white-fronted geese, and many other species.

13

THE FAT OF THE LAND

Farming has been a traditional occupation in Ireland because of the fertile soil and mild climate. Regular rainfall means that little irrigation (watering of crops) is needed.

Once, landlords rented out their small, not very profitable farms to tenants. In the west there are still many small farms. In the midlands and east, where the land is more productive, the farms are bigger (often over 16 square miles). Small and medium-sized farms usually raise many different varieties of crops and animals, and sell their produce at local markets. Large farms tend to be more mechanized and specialize in producing one or two crops, such as wheat, or livestock. They export their produce or sell it to markets a distance away.

Rich pastures provide grazing for beef cattle, sheep, horses, and, most of all, dairy cows. Butter, cheese, and yogurt are products of the dairy industry.

Once, nearly every Irish cottager owned a pig and some chickens. Many pigs are still raised, especially in the south and west, as well as poultry. Potatoes, sugar beet, turnips, and rutabagas are the chief root crops grown. The main cereals are wheat, barley, and oats.

In parts of Ireland crops are still harvested by hand, but since Ireland joined the European Economic Community (EEC) in 1973, more money has been available for farming. Now, on the larger farms, the most modern methods and machines are used.

Milk production

Although some dairy herds are quite large, average-sized Irish farms have about 20 cows. Farmers with small farms cannot afford to buy much winter feed. Milk production is therefore much greater in the summer months, when grazing is best. Milk is collected from the farms daily.

Crofters

A croft is a small enclosed plot of land, adjoining a house, which is worked by the renter, known as a crofter, and his family. There are still many crofters in the west of Ireland. Some of their land is used for crops, some for grazing, and some for cutting turf for fuel. In the summer, crofters may work as fishermen or in other jobs.

Cereal crops

Wheat and oats are important cereal crops. Barley, which is grown to make beer and whiskey, is another important crop. Harvesting can be a difficult time for Irish farmers because of the damp weather.

FROM THE SOIL AND THE SEA

Recently, some useful finds of minerals such as lead and zinc have been made in Ireland, although on the whole the country is not very rich in minerals. It has little coal or iron ore, though it does have oil and gas, mainly off the coast.

Since prehistoric times, the Irish have used peat from the bogs for fuel. Peat bogs cover nearly 20 percent of the land surface. Peat is formed over a very long time from rotting vegetation. It is cut into pieces, called sods, and dried. Then it can be burned like coal or wood. Several power stations have been built that burn peat to generate electricity. Peat is also cheap: oil costs ten times as much.

The Irish also get electric power from their rivers. Hydroelectric plants, which generate power by the force of flowing water, have been built on the Shannon and other rivers.

Around the coasts and the offshore islands, many people make a living from fishing. Cod, skate, flounder, herring, mackerel, and other fish are caught, especially off the west coast. There are no big fleets of trawlers, though, and Irish fishermen are worried that foreign fleets may spoil their fishing waters by removing too many fish.

Cutting peat
Peat is still sometimes cut by hand, using special long-bladed spades like the one shown above. Nowadays, though, machines are more often used. The first job, and it's a hard one to do with a spade, is to dig ditches and channels, like the one on the left, to drain the bog.

The top layer of a peat bog is too light to make good fuel, but it is very useful in gardens, to improve the soil. Ireland exports hundreds of tons of this agricultural peat, but all fuel peat is used in Ireland.

Fishing for a living

Fishing boats look for fish and shellfish around the Irish coast and the offshore islands. This picture shows boats at Dingle harbor, in southwest Ireland. Shellfish provide the tastiest dishes in many Irish restaurants, but on the east coast, pollution is a growing danger.

Fish farming

Fish farming, mainly shellfish and salmon, is becoming a large industry in Ireland. The finger-sized young salmon are raised in huge wire enclosures around the coasts.

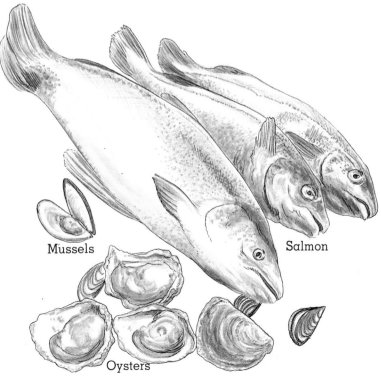

Mussels

Salmon

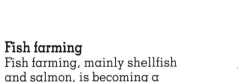

Oysters

WORKSHOP AND FACTORY

I reland has little heavy industry, except in Northern Ireland, where Belfast is a big industrial city. Even in Belfast the old industries like shipbuilding are not as important as they once were. Light manufacturing industries, such as those that produce food, electronic goods, and chemicals, have been growing in recent years, especially around Dublin, Cork, Limerick, and other large towns.

The great problem for Irish industry has always been lack of money for investment, but more money has become available since Ireland joined the EEC. Today the state plays a large part in industry, running many big concerns, while others are owned by private companies.

Some of the old Irish industries have faded, but the brewing of a type of beer called stout and the distilling of Irish whiskey are still booming. Linen, another traditional industry, has almost disappeared, but Donegal tweed and Aran Island sweaters are still made. New clothing factories use imported materials, such as Australian wool and manmade textiles. About three million pairs of shoes are made in Ireland every year.

The new electronics industry alone has provided about 20,000 jobs in the past 20 years, but Irish unemployment is still high. Nearly one in every five workers has no regular job.

KEY FACTS

▶ The government aids industry through the IDA (Industrial Development Authority), which has helped make 50,000 new jobs in the past 15 years.
▶ The government also tries to attract foreign business to Ireland. The biggest overseas investor is the U.S., which has more than 300 companies based in Ireland.
▶ Electronics (computers, etc.) is the fastest-growing industry. It provides about 20 percent of Irish exports (measured by value).
▶ The main products are food, electronic goods, chemicals, and textiles.
▶ More Irish goods are sold to Britain than to any other country.
▶ The tourist industry is one of the Republic's largest sources of income, and it is expanding rapidly. Popular tourist areas include the Lakes of Killarney and the west coast.

Sugar beet
Ireland makes most of its own sugar from home-grown sugar beet. Its sugar factories produce enough for export as well.

Linen- and glass-making

Among the oldest Irish industries are linen- and glass-making. Linen is a small business now, but glass is still one of Ireland's most famous products. It was first made in Waterford over 200 years ago. Today the Waterford Crystal Company (left) employs more than 3,000 people. Some pieces of Waterford glass cost thousands of dollars.

Irish industry

The port of Waterford on the Suir River is convenient for local industry. Goods can be transported from Irish ports to Europe and other export markets.

AROUND IRELAND

The Republic of Ireland has a good system of roads and, except around cities in the rush hour, no traffic jams! There are fewer cars per mile than in most other European countries, and in some rural districts the motorists wave to every passing car. Smaller roads are often rough; some of them carry more sheep and cows than cars and trucks.

However, traffic has grown in recent times and, as a result, many small railroad lines have been closed. The main lines mostly run to and from Dublin. The national transportation company, the CIE, runs both railroads and buses. Buses run frequently even in quite deserted parts of Ireland.

The main international airport is Shannon, near Limerick in the west. There are also airports at Dublin, Cork, Galway, Sligo, and other centers. Aer Lingus, the national airline, flies to about 30 international airports and carries two and a half million passengers a year.

Hundreds of people cross the Irish Sea to Britain every day. Many Irish men and women travel to work in England and home for holidays throughout the year, and in the summer tourists raise the numbers. The state-owned B & I shipping line carries one million passengers, 150,000 cars, and two million tons of cargo every year. That is only one-third of the total traffic between Ireland and Britain.

Jaunting car
The two-wheeled jaunting car is a traditional Irish vehicle. One hundred years ago it was the most common form of transportation. Today a few are kept to give rides to the tourists.

Dun Laoghaire
At the port of Dun Laoghaire (pronounced Doon Leary), 8 miles from Dublin, the big ferries take people and cargo to Britain and the continent. The harbor of Dun Laoghaire is also the home of many yachts.

Irish railroads

This train is standing at Bray station, in the east of Ireland near Dublin. Long-distance trains are drawn by diesel engines. Suburban trains are electric.

Shannon

Most of the big European and American airlines fly to Shannon, which, pilots say, is one of the safest airports in the world.

CELTIC KINGDOM

I reland is rich in prehistoric monuments, some of which are even older than the Celts, the people who settled there about 2,500 years ago. The Celts formed small kingdoms, ruled by local kings and druids, or wise men. Unlike England, Ireland was never conquered by the Romans, so the Irish Celts were able to develop their own society and traditions.

In the 5th century St. Patrick came to Ireland and established Christianity. He was followed by other saints, like St. Brendan and St. Bridget, and many monasteries were built. During Europe's "dark ages," after the end of the Roman Empire, Ireland was probably the most civilized country in Europe. It was "a land of saints and scholars," and Irish missionaries helped keep Christianity alive on the continent.

The peaceful Irish monasteries suffered when the Viking invasions began, before 800. The monks built tall round towers (many are still standing) to keep themselves and their treasures safe. After some time the invaders began to make settlements, and founded city-ports like Dublin, Cork, Waterford, and Wexford. When new invasions began, Brian Boru, the Irish king, defeated the Vikings once and for all at the battle of Clontarf in 1014.

Druids
There may have been druids among the earliest Irish people, even before the Celts arrived. They were like the elders of a tribe, or wise men, who knew about law and religion. They also claimed to have magic powers. When Ireland turned to Christianity, they became less important.

Ancient Ireland
The seat of the Irish kings was at Tara. Because the buildings were wooden and did not last, only earthworks can be seen now. There were several kingdoms — sometimes five, at other times seven — in ancient Ireland, and the king never controlled the whole country. He was a symbolic leader of the nation.

The Book of Kells

The Book of Kells is Ireland's greatest treasure. It is an illustrated copy of the Gospels in Latin, made by monks over 1,200 years ago. Art experts say it is the finest example of the early Christian art of illuminated (or decorated) manuscripts. Today it can be seen in the library of Trinity College, Dublin.

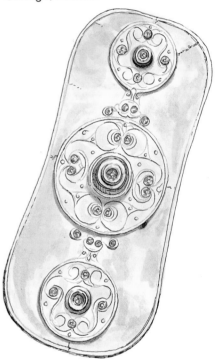

Celtic shield

Celtic brooch

The Tara Brooch

Celtic art

Celtic art used many beautiful abstract designs. The Celts were especially good at metalwork. The 8th-century Tara Brooch is one of the finest examples of Celtic art.

23

ENGLISH COLONY

I n 1152 the King of Leinster needed help in a quarrel with his neighbor. He asked Henry II, the King of England, to allow him to use some nobles from England to assist him. In 1170 Henry II himself invaded Ireland with an army, and a 400-year struggle for control of the country began. This constant fighting almost brought Ireland to ruin.

The English only controlled an area around Dublin, known as the Pale, until the powerful Tudor dynasty came to the English throne. Under Elizabeth I (who reigned from 1558 to 1603) the Irish were finally conquered, and in the 17th century many English and Scottish settlers moved to Ireland, especially Ulster. These settlers were mostly Protestants.

England had become Protestant under the Tudors, but the Irish remained Catholics. In the English Civil War (1642-1651) the Irish supported the king against the stern Protestantism of Oliver Cromwell. So Cromwell invaded Ireland, destroying towns, burning farms, and slaughtering people.

In 1688 the Irish again supported the Catholic king, James II, against the Protestant William III. James took refuge in Ireland, but William defeated him at the Battle of the Boyne in 1690.

The British treated the Irish harshly, preventing them from voting or owning land, and a rebellion in 1798 was fiercely crushed. The Act of Union (1800) abolished Ireland's parliament, but in 1829 the great leader of the Catholic Irish, Daniel O'Connell, won the right of Catholics to be members of the British parliament.

The Battle of the Boyne (1690)
This battle ended all hopes for a Catholic king or queen and caused great rejoicing in Protestant parts of Ulster. Even now, 300 years later, there is still much ill-feeling between Catholics and Protestants over this battle. On July 12 there are annual marches throughout Northern Ireland to commemorate the battle.

Trinity College, Dublin

Trinity College, Dublin, was founded in the 16th century, with the agreement of Elizabeth I. Catholics were not allowed to teach there until 1871. Its great library, like the university libraries of Oxford and Cambridge, receives a copy of every book published in Great Britain and Ireland.

Anglo-Normans

The 12th-century invaders of Ireland are called Anglo-("English") Normans. Remains of Anglo-Norman castles, such as Carrickfergus Castle in County Antrim, can still be seen in Ireland.

The Anglo-Irish

The English settlers and their descendants built fine houses for themselves in the Irish countryside. Muckross House, shown here, is such a house in County Kerry. Dublin too became a very elegant city in the 18th century, thanks to Irish and British architects.

THE GREAT HUNGER

I n the past most Irish people had very little money. They lived mainly on a diet based on potatoes. From 1845 to 1847 disease destroyed the potato crops. Thousands of people died of starvation because they couldn't obtain other food. Others managed to leave the country. The population fell from 8.5 million to 5.5 million in 10 years. This disaster was blamed on the British government.

The Irish, led by Charles Stewart Parnell, wanted "Home Rule" — their own parliament for governing Irish affairs — but not complete independence. A smaller, secret group, the Fenians, or Irish Republican Brotherhood (IRB), wanted a separate Irish state.

Conditions in Ireland began to improve at last. The British government reformed the laws, which meant that people in the west were able to buy their farms from the landlords. By 1910 the Liberal government was ready to give Ireland Home Rule. This was fiercely opposed by the Ulster Protestants, known as Unionists, who wished to remain part of the United Kingdom. Then came World War 1, and the question of Home Rule was put aside in Britain.

At Easter 1916 a group led by the IRB staged an uprising in Dublin. The uprising was soon crushed and its leaders shot by the British. It seemed to have been a complete failure, but it was the spark that ignited Ireland. After 1916 Home Rule was dead and forgotten. A new movement, called *Sinn Fein* ("Ourselves"), whose aim was complete independence, arose in Ireland.

Charles Stewart Parnell (1846-1891)
Though a Protestant of Anglo-Irish descent, Parnell was the champion of his country in the battle for Home Rule. He was known as the "uncrowned king of Ireland."

The Potato Famine
In the late 1840s about one million Irish people died of starvation during the Famine. A disease called potato blight destroyed the potatoes people lived on. The British government reduced the price of bread, but too late to be of much help. The people had so little money that they had to bury their dead without coffins.

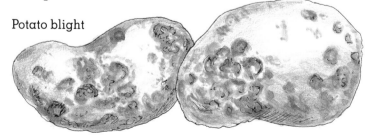

Potato blight

Homeless

People who could not pay their rent were thrown out of their cottages. If they resisted, the buildings were knocked down. Violence became widespread. Some cruel land agents, acting for the landlords who lived elsewhere, were murdered.

Leave or starve

The choice that faced many people in 19th-century Ireland was to leave or starve. Between 1841 and 1925 over five million people emigrated to North America. Others went to Britain and Australasia.

THE ORANGE AND THE GREEN

I n a general election in 1918 the Sinn Fein party won a huge victory. Most members were in prison, but the rest set up an independent Irish parliament, Dáil Éireann. Eamon de Valera escaped from an English prison and was elected president of an Irish Republic.

The struggle for independence from Britain had begun. The chief Irish armed force was the Irish Republican Army (IRA). The British used a force known as the Black and Tans, so-called because of the color of their uniforms. For three years both sides carried out brutal acts of terrorism and murder.

In 1921 a treaty was signed in London that created the Irish Free State. It gave Ireland self-government, but not complete independence. It also left out the six Protestant counties of Northern Ireland. Their leader, Edward Carson, had gained a promise from the British government that they would not have to join with the Catholic southern Irish.

Michael Collins, hero of the war against the British, and most members of the Dáil supported the treaty, but many Republicans did not. Civil war began again — a "War of the Brothers" in which those who had fought together against the British now fought each other.

De Valera helped end this bitter war. He led the country to true independence under a new constitution that declared Ireland a republic in 1949. Today the aim of the government of the Republic is to unite Ireland, to include both Northern Ireland and the Republic. However, terrorism and local civil war in the north make any solution to the problem difficult to reach.

Eamon de Valera (1882-1975)
The father of modern Ireland, Eamon de Valera, was sentenced to death after the Easter Rising, but reprieved. Later, as prime minister, he tried to remove the traces of British influence from Irish life. He encouraged Irish customs and traditions, especially the Irish language.

Steps to independence

1916 Irish republic proclaimed in Easter Rising crushed by the British.
1918 Sinn Fein wins 73 seats in election.
1919 Dáil Éireann set up. Revolt against Britain.
1921 Irish Free State Treaty.
1932 Eamon de Valera becomes prime minister.
1937 New constitution ending British ties.
1949 Act of British parliament recognizes the Irish Republic as a state outside the Commonwealth.

GPO, O'Connell Street, Dublin

English soldiers inside the remains of the General Post Office in O'Connell Street, Dublin, in 1916. This was the nationalist headquarters during the Easter Rising. It was destroyed by British gunboats firing from the Liffey River, and later rebuilt. (Inset) — The building as it is today.

Dublin Castle

This was the headquarters of British authority in Ireland. Today it contains government offices. The grand state apartments are open to the public.

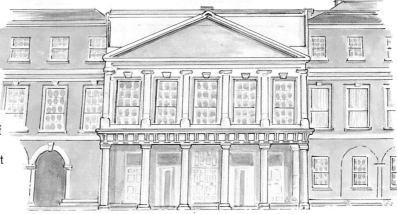

RUNNING THE COUNTRY

The head of state in the Irish Republic is the president, who is elected every seven years. He has more power than the Queen of England, but less power than an American president. The head of government is the prime minister, or Taoiseach. Although he is appointed by the president, the president does not choose the Taoiseach, who must be recommended by the parliament, known as the Dáil.

The Dáil has 166 elected members, and the Senate has 60 members. Unlike the president and the Dáil, the Senate is not elected by popular vote (the vote of all adult citizens). Eleven senators are chosen by the Taoiseach. The rest are elected by the Dáil and by groups representing parts of society, such as education and industry.

There are two main political parties. Fianna Fail, the party of De Valera, usually has most seats and therefore most often forms the government. Fine Gael sometimes forms a government with the aid of small parties, such as Labour. Socialist parties have never done well in Ireland, mainly because they get no support from the Church.

EEC membership
The Republic of Ireland joined the European Economic Community (EEC) in 1973. In the early years Ireland gained great benefits from membership through grants and subsidies. More recently, the benefits have been smaller.

Irish parliament
The Irish parliament has two houses (like the U.S. Congress and the British parliament). The lower house, Dáil Éireann, is more important than the Senate, or Seanad Éireann.

The Four Courts

This is the legal heart of the Republic. Its famous dome had to be rebuilt after it was severely damaged during the fight for independence from Britain. The building actually contains many more than four law courts.

Political differences

Lively political debates take place in the Dáil. The differences between the two largest parties, however, are not very great. In foreign policy, Fianna Fáil has usually been more anti-British. Here, Charles Haughey (left), Prime Minister and leader of Fianna Fáil, and Dr. Garret Fitzgerald (right) shake hands before the start of a television debate.

RELIGION IN IRELAND

For centuries the Roman Catholic Church has been a powerful influence on the Irish people. Their Catholic faith strengthened their resistance to British rule, when the official religion was Protestant and Catholics were not allowed to vote or own land. Even today the leading person in country districts is often the parish priest. There are few Protestants left in the Republic, except around Dublin; about 93 percent of the people are Catholics. Nearly 20,000 are priests, nuns, monks, or brothers.

Although the Catholic Church no longer has a special place in the Irish Constitution, its influence is reflected in law and government. For example, divorce is not allowed in the Republic except in a few cases, because the Catholic Church (and the constitution) forbids it.

The head of the Roman Catholic Church in Ireland is the archbishop of Armagh, which is in Northern Ireland. There the situation is different, because two-thirds of the people are Protestants. Some belong to the Church of Ireland, which is Anglican like the Church of England. But a larger number are Presbyterians. Hostility between Protestants and Roman Catholics, caused by events over the last 500 years, is one of the main causes of the violence in Northern Ireland.

Celtic cross
There are still a few Celtic crosses standing today. These were made in the great days of the Celtic Church, more than 1,000 years ago.

Religious sites
Shrines, containing a statue of the Virgin Mary, are often seen by the roadside in Ireland. The one shown here is next to a well.

Schools and schooling

The Catholic religious orders play a large part in education. Many Irish politicians and officials went to schools run by the Christian Brothers. This order was founded in 1802 to help poor Catholic boys at a time when Catholic schools were not allowed.

Mass and pilgrimages

Most families go to Mass on Sundays. Priests have been powerful figures in Ireland and play an important part in the community.

Many people go on pilgrimages, such as these people who are praying on Mount Patrick.

IRISH EDUCATION AND LANGUAGE

All children in the Irish Republic must go to school between the ages of 6 and 15. Nearly all elementary schools (for children up to age 12) are run by the state and are free. After the first year boys and girls go to separate classes. There are special classes for slow learners and for children of "travelers" (the people once called "tinkers" who do not live in one place for very long but travel around the country, like gypsies).

Secondary schools are private, but they are assisted by state grants. In many schools the teachers are nuns or brothers. The state also gives grants to non-Catholic children to attend non-Catholic schools.

The oldest university is the University of Dublin, better known as Trinity College. It was founded nearly 400 years ago. The National University of Ireland, founded in 1909, has colleges in Dublin, Cork, and Galway. The older college of St. Patrick, Maynooth, is also now part of the National University.

The government has tried very hard to encourage the Irish language. However, because of television and tourism, more Irish people speak English today than in 1921. Even in the Gaeltacht (see page 10), everyone now understands English.

The Irish language
Irish (Gaelic) is the first official language. All children must learn it. In some elementary schools all lessons are taught in Irish.

To class on time

Many Irish children live in scattered Irish villages in the country, so they often have to travel a long way to school. School buses like the one shown here make long tours round the countryside collecting all the children.

Gaelic, the living language

The widespread use of Irish can be seen on all street names, public notices, and signposts which are printed in Irish and English. Irish Gaelic and Scottish Gaelic were once the same language. (The Scots originally came from Ireland.) They have developed differently, but today one who speaks Irish can read a book in Scottish Gaelic without too much trouble.

THE WRITTEN WORD

In the Irish Republic, writers, like artists and composers, may not have to pay income tax on their work. This is a sign of the high position literature has held in Ireland during the last 300 years. It is said that Irish people write as easily as they read.

There have been great Gaelic writers, but few non-Irish people could read their works. These writers did not become famous until their works were translated into English and other languages.

In the 19th century a great revival of Irish culture began. This revival was linked to the rise of Irish nationalism. For the first time Irish writers (writing in English) began to describe Irish subjects, Irish traditions, Irish people, and Irish problems. A leading figure in this revival was William Butler Yeats. With Lady Gregory he created the famous Abbey Theatre in Dublin.

There were still other great Irish writers, such as Oscar Wilde and George Bernard Shaw, who did not write much about Ireland. Today there are probably more novelists, poets, and playwrights in Ireland, compared with the whole population, than in any other English-speaking country.

Irish media
Ireland has four national newspapers, including the famous *Irish Times* and *Cork Examiner*. There are also many local papers. The national broadcasting company (RTE) runs two television channels and three radio stations (one broadcasts only in Irish).

Symbol of the national broadcasting company

The Abbey Theatre

The Abbey Theatre, in Dublin, was at the heart of the literary revival in Ireland around the beginning of this century.

Irish literary giants of the past 100 years

Oscar Wilde (1854-1900), playwright and critic, author of brilliant comedies.

William Butler Yeats (1865-1939), poet, playwright, and leader of the Anglo-Irish revival.

James Joyce (1882-1941), Dublin novelist who had enormous influence on literary style.

George Bernard Shaw (1856-1950), a wise and witty playwright, critic, and novelist.

Sean O'Casey (1884-1964), playwright who wrote about the "Troubles" of the civil war, and the Dublin slums.

Samuel Beckett (born 1906), playwright whose plays, written in French and English, are about human loneliness.

37

MUSIC AND THE ARTS

One of the symbols of Ireland is the harp, which was played many hundreds of years ago by the Celtic bards (poet-singers). Traditional Irish music is very popular today, and not only in Ireland. Although few people play the harp, you can still hear the Irish bagpipes, tin whistle, fiddle, and *bodhran* (a drum like a large tambourine). The old songs were written in Irish, of course, but in the many "music pubs" of modern Ireland they are often sung in English. Each region has its own style of folk music, but many of the finest songs come from the southwest.

Old songs are still popular in Ireland, but the Irish also like other kinds of music. In Wexford in October there is an opera festival; an annual jazz festival is held in Cork; and Irish pop singers (like U2 and Bob Geldof) are known all over the world.

Dublin is especially famous for its theater and its buildings. Much of the city was built in the 18th century (the Georgian period), when architecture was especially elegant. Besides Georgian Dublin, the Anglo-Irish built fine country houses. Many of these are now open to the public, along with old castles, abbeys, and gardens.

Belleek
Belleek is a little village in Ulster. It is so close to the border of Northern Ireland that people say you can hook a salmon in the river in the Republic and land it in Northern Ireland. Since 1857 Belleek has been famous for a special kind of ornamental porcelain (china), which is still made today. It has a pearly appearance, and some pieces are extremely fine and fragile.

Irish pipes
A musician in traditional dress playing the Irish pipes. They are similar to Scottish bagpipes, but are inflated by bellows held beneath the arm rather than by a blow-pipe.

The Custom House

One of Dublin's most attractive buildings, this was designed in the 1780s by James Gandon, Ireland's finest achitect. He also built the Four Courts (see page 31).

Traditional folksongs

Folksingers keep alive the old airs, jigs, laments, ballads, and reels. The government has also helped, especially through *Radio na Gaeltachta*, the Irish-language radio station. Some of the songs heard in villages today have never been written down.

FROM FOOTBALL TO FISHING

During the rise of Irish national spirit in the late 19th century, the Gaelic Athletic Association (G.A.A.) worked hard to revive traditional Irish games, which are now very popular.

Hurling is a fast, fierce game, like a mixture of hockey and lacrosse. The ball may be kicked, caught by hand, or hurled through the air or along the ground with a curved bat called a hurley.

In Gaelic football, the ball is kicked, punched, or carried. Like other forms of football, it once was a village free-for-all until the G.A.A. gave it strict rules.

International games like soccer and rugby are played to the highest level, and Irish golfers have made a world-famous name for themselves.

Horses seem to hold a special place in Ireland. The Curragh, a grassy region of drained bog to the southwest of Dublin, is the home of Irish horse racing. Irish racehorses are exported to all parts of the world.

Ireland is a paradise for fishermen. The rivers are less polluted than most, and many contain salmon and sea trout, as well as native brown trout. Fishing for freshwater and sea fish is a very popular sport and attracts many visitors to the country.

Going fishing
Salmon and trout attract many fishermen to Ireland's lakes and rivers. According to legend, the lakes also contain monster pike. There are stories of fish more than 88 pounds in weight being caught in Lough Derg and the Shannon River.

Irish racehorses
The green grass of the Curragh covers about 8 square miles. It grows on a limestone plain, and is said to raise horses with strong bones. The success of Irish racehorses, at home and abroad, depends mainly on the skill and knowledge of the breeders.

Hurling

Hurling is especially popular in the south, and the provinces of Leinster and Munster are keen rivals. Crowds of more than 70,000 people watch the annual All-Ireland final in Croke Park, Dublin.

Gaelic football

In this game the ball is round, as in soccer, but the goalposts are H-shaped, as in football. To score one point, the ball must pass between the posts and over the crossbar. If it is kicked or punched under the crossbar, three points are scored.

EVERYDAY LIFE

The sense of community in Ireland is still strong, especially in the countryside. The center of everyday life is the family, and families are often large. Until a few years ago, Irish girls expected to get married and to spend their lives looking after husband, home, and children. Today, more married women have jobs.

Although prices in food stores are quite high, Irish people eat more frozen and packaged food than they once did. Yet, as a farming country, Ireland produces excellent food. Beef, lamb, ham, bacon, butter, eggs, and seafood are especially good. A typical Irish supper might be bacon cooked with cabbage or potato cakes, or Irish stew, which is made of mutton, onions, and potatoes. Another Irish favorite, though more expensive, is poached salmon.

The growing number of people who live in towns can spend weekends and vacations enjoying outdoor activities in the beautiful countryside. Besides lakes and mountains, there is also the beautiful Irish coastline.

On two wheels
Ireland is a pleasant country for bicycling. The roads are not crowded, and the tall hedges that line them are full of small animals and birds. More people use bicycles than cars for traveling short distances.

By the seaside

No location in Ireland is more than 68 miles from the sea. Along the almost 3,100 miles of coast are many wide, sandy beaches, which do not get too crowded, even in the height of summer.

Daily bread

Many people still do their own baking. The nutty-tasting, slightly sour soda bread, which this woman is making, is delicious. So is barm brack, a rich, fruity loaf.

THE FUTURE IN IRELAND

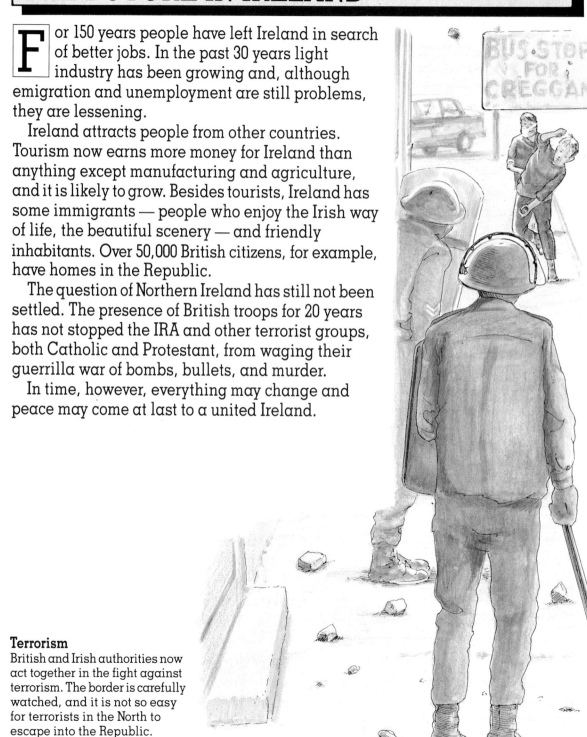

For 150 years people have left Ireland in search of better jobs. In the past 30 years light industry has been growing and, although emigration and unemployment are still problems, they are lessening.

Ireland attracts people from other countries. Tourism now earns more money for Ireland than anything except manufacturing and agriculture, and it is likely to grow. Besides tourists, Ireland has some immigrants — people who enjoy the Irish way of life, the beautiful scenery — and friendly inhabitants. Over 50,000 British citizens, for example, have homes in the Republic.

The question of Northern Ireland has still not been settled. The presence of British troops for 20 years has not stopped the IRA and other terrorist groups, both Catholic and Protestant, from waging their guerrilla war of bombs, bullets, and murder.

In time, however, everything may change and peace may come at last to a united Ireland.

Terrorism
British and Irish authorities now act together in the fight against terrorism. The border is carefully watched, and it is not so easy for terrorists in the North to escape into the Republic.

Blarney Castle

Blarney Castle is one of the popular tourist attractions that brings visitors and money to Ireland. According to legend, if you kiss the Blarney Stone (a stone slab on the battlements) you will receive the "gift of the gab" and become a good talker.

An industrial future

In the past 30 years Ireland has become the base for many new industries. Old industries are also up-to-date. The Guinness brewery in Dublin (shown here), which has long produced one of Ireland's most famous exports (the dark beer known as stout), uses the most advanced methods available. More than 50,000 people visit the Guinness Museum every year, and many more people enjoy the drink itself.

Index

Acknowledgments

Map by Ann Savage. All other illustrations by Borin van Loon. Photographic credits (a = above, b = below, m = middle, l = left, r = right): Cover al J. Allan Cash Ltd; bl Sunak/Zefa; ar Hutchison Library; br Robert Harding Picture Library; page 8 Hed Wiesner/Zefa; page 10 Zefa; page 11 Northern Ireland Tourist Board; page 21 Pat O'Dea/ Irish Tourist Board; page 13 Eichhorn/Z./Zefa; page 15 a H. Schmied/Zefa, b Jon Gardey/Robert Harding Picture Library; page 16 Trevor Wood/Robert Harding Picture Library; page 17 Zefa; page 19 a Robert Harding Picture Library, b Nick Holt/Zefa; page 20 Brian Lynch/Irish Tourist Board; page 21 a P. Moszynski/Hutchison Library, b Zefa – Pfaff; page 22 Brian Lynch/Irish Tourist Board; page 23 Bridgeman Art Library; page 25 a Hutchison Library, m Zefa, b J. Allan Cash Ltd; page 29 a Hulton Picture Library, b Paddy Tutty/ Irish Tourist Board; page 30 Irish Tourist Board; page 31 Robert Harding Picture Library; page 33 Robert Harding Picture Library; page 35 Paddy Tutty/Irish Tourist Board; page 37 Earl Young/Robert Harding Picture Library; page 38 Northern Ireland Tourist Board; page 39 Paddy Tutty/Irish Tourist Board; page 40 a Pat O'Dea/Irish Tourist Board, b Paddy Tutty/Irish Tourist Board; page 41 Irish Tourist Board; page 43 Robert Harding Picture Library; page 45 a Gascoigne/Robert Harding Picture Library, b J. Allan Cash Ltd.